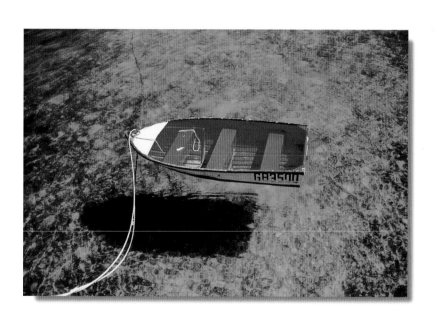

"My total dedication and obsession
with photography has taken me
on journeys into many remarkable
areas throughout Australia.
I captured this collection of images
using a specialist panoramic camera.
Because of the wider field of view,
this format enables me to portray
the true spirit of Australia
on film. Upon viewing these images
I am sure you will share with me
the tranquillity and solitude
I experienced whilst exploring the
stunning beauty of this country."

www.peterlikimages.com

PO Box 2529 Cairns Queensland 4870 Australia
Telephone: (07) 4053 9000 **Fax:** (07) 4032 1277
sales@peterlik.com.au   **www.peterlik.com.au**

© **Peter Lik Publishing**   BK07

ISBN 0 9 47163 43 3

Front cover - Burleigh Heads looking towards Surfers Paradise
Back cover - Main Beach at daybreak
Additional photography - Murray Waite & Associates,
                                            Tourism Queensland.

GOLD COAST

Queensland's Gold Coast, about an hour's drive south of Brisbane, is a region of contrasts. With Surfers Paradise as its hub it stretches south to the New South Wales border along 42 kilometres of golden beaches, and west to the lush subtropical hinterland.

With a permanent population of approximately 400,000 people, the Gold Coast attracts nearly four million tourists each year. Not only do they come to enjoy the beaches, the pleasant climate with 300 days of sunshine a year and the scenery, but also the wide range of accommodation and entertainment designed to suit every taste.

The Gold Coast offers a variety of entertainment - there are shopping malls, coffee shops, restaurants, discos, live bands, theatres, nightclubs, Jupiters Casino, theme parks such as Movieworld, Dreamworld, Sea World, Wet 'n Wild, flora and fauna parks such as Currumbin Sanctuary and Fleay's Fauna Centre. The Gold Coast also offers a range of sporting activities for all age groups.

While Surfers Paradise, with its highrise development, is the focal point of the Gold Coast, a few blocks back from the beach is the Nerang River with its network of canals. Many permanent residents live along these canals with their private jetties - a popular retirement area for Southerners. Further west is the McPherson Range and Lamington National Park which form the largest preserved subtropical rainforest in Australia with 160 kilometres of walking tracks.

Between the mainland and South Stradbroke Island is the Broadwater, a calm stretch of water used by yachts and power boats throughout the year.

Tourists and locals create a colourful collage on the world-famous Surfers Paradise beach.

Another perfect day at Tallebudgera Creek.

Surfers Paradise.

Overleaf: Aerial view of Coolangatta and Tweed Heads.

A panoramic view from Burleigh Heads looking north towards Surfers Paradise.

Dawn at Surfers Paradise Beach, one of the world's best beaches.

The turquoise waves of the Pacific Ocean caress the pristine white sands of Surfers Paradise Beach.

Twilight reflections on the Nerang River, Surfers Paradise.

Sunset over the Southport Broadwater.

Chevron Renaissance, a shopper's paradise.

Twilight over the night markets - where local handcrafts and arts can be bargained for.

The internationally-acclaimed Conrad Jupiters Hotel and Casino.

Pacific Fair Shopping Centre.

Palazzo Versace and Marina Mirage.

Previous page: Aerial panoramic vista of Main Beach, the Broadwater and Surfers Paradise.

The sparkling Gold Coast city lights reflected on the sands of Surfers Paradise Beach.

The crystal waters of Greenmount Beach, one of Australia's finest beaches.

Spectacular night lights of the Gold Coast Highway run through the heart of Surfers Paradise.

The dedicated muscular Gold Coast lifesavers ensure the safety of millions of visitors each year.

The pristine beaches are the ultimate playground for all water sports.

Sunrise greets the morning catch.

Tedder Avenue, Main Beach boasts many fine restaurants.

Reflections at dusk over the Jubilee Bridge, gateway to Surfers Paradise.

The Broadwater, a boating paradise.

HINTERLAND

*B*ehind the busy Gold Coast strip lies the hinterland - another world with rainforest clad peaks, stunning waterfalls and amazing lookouts. You can stay in secluded huts situated in Lamington National Park at O'Reilly's or Binna Burra and trek for days to discover this World Heritage wilderness on your own. You may encounter rare song birds, green tree frogs and the amazing Antarctic beech trees which live for over 3000 years.

At Mount Tamborine, Curtis Falls quietly cascade through a magnificent palm-lined valley where you can have devonshire tea amongst this beauty. Various lookouts near Mount Tamborine offer spectacular views over the McPherson ranges and valleys lined with crystal clear streams.

In Springbrook National Park the magnificent natural arch waterfall cascades through a collapsed section of cave - one of the most beautiful scenes in Australia.

The koala is one of the attractions at Currumbin Sanctuary.

Overleaf: 3000 year old Antarctic beech trees, Lamington National Park.

A Rainbow Lorikeet displays his fluorescent colours.

Elbana Falls cascade through the lush rainforest of Lamington National Park.

The golden bower bird and white lipped tree frog are two of the most famous inhabitants of the mystical rainforest of Lamington National Park.

Classic country panoramic vistas at Lower Beechmont.

Early morning mist over Egg Rock, an outstanding feature below Lamington National Park.

The incredible phenomenon of the natural arch, where a sunlit curtain of water cascades into a precipitous cave, Numinbah Valley.

Curtis Falls, one of the most picturesque waterfalls at Mt Tamborine.

Sweet dreams at Dreamworld with Kenny and Belinda.

Extreme dreams on the Tower of Terror.

Wild dreams at Dreamworld.

Warner Bros. Movie World, Hollywood on the Gold Coast features the famous dynamic duo - Batman & Robin.

You can meet the world's most loved characters at Warner Bros. Movie World.

The unique Lethal Weapon Ride at Warner Bros. Movie World.

Wet 'n' Wild Water World combines all the fun and excitement of the world's latest water slides and leisure pools.

Ping Ping and Kanook, stars of Polar Bear Shores, Sea World.

Another perfect day in Currumbin Creek.

Aerial view of Bond University.

Aerial view of Sanctuary Cove, host to one of the biggest on-water boat shows in the southern Hemisphere.

The Gold Coast was first outside America to host a leg of the Indy Car Series, now an annual event.

The Surfers Paradise party continues after dark.

Shop 'till you drop at Robina Town Centre.

Aerial view of Broadbeach.

Overleaf: The crystal clear waters of Coolangatta are enjoyed by sunseekers all year round.

The azure waters of the Pacific Ocean lap the shores of Greenmount Beach.

Rainbow Bay, Queensland's southern-most beach.

Overleaf: Gold Coast tranquillity.

Peter Lik Gallery

Multi award-winning photographer Peter Lik proudly
presents his signature Galleries. The Galleries,
with their handcrafted timber floors and unique
custom decor radiate a beautiful ambience.

The stunning 'Gallery Collection' is selected from
Peter's library of over 250,000 images and hand
printed as limited edition Ilfochrome photographs.

Entering a Peter Lik Gallery is a total sensory
experience. His connection with the heart and
soul of the landscape is evident and he captures
the true feeling of the land like no other.